IMAGES
of America

BENTONVILLE
BATTLEFIELD STATE
HISTORIC SITE

In March 2022, Bentonville Battlefield State Historic Site, in collaboration with the Friends of Bentonville Battlefield, presented "Peace to the Gallant Dead" in commemoration of the battle's 157th anniversary. Volunteers placed 4,133 luminaria in a field adjacent to the Harper House, one for each casualty of the battle. This incredible spectacle allowed for some comprehension of how large the number 4,133 truly is and how savage the battle was. (Greg Stevens.)

ON THE COVER: During a tour of Bentonville led by historian Fred Olds, an unidentified visitor aims a musket at another visitor in this 1927 photograph. The visitors stand near the newly erected monument to the North Carolina Junior Reserves with a billboard map behind them. The fields and forests that still dominated Bentonville are visible in the background. (North Carolina Museum of History.)

IMAGES
of America

BENTONVILLE
BATTLEFIELD STATE
HISTORIC SITE

Colby Lipscomb and Derrick Brown
Foreword by Wade Sokolosky

ARCADIA
PUBLISHING

Published by Arcadia Publishing
Charleston, South Carolina

Printed in the United States of America

Library of Congress Control Number: 2023952496

For all general information, please contact Arcadia Publishing:
Telephone 843-853-2070
Fax 843-853-0044
E-mail sales@arcadiapublishing.com

Visit us on the Internet at www.arcadiapublishing.com

To Donny Taylor and Tim Westbrook, who are sitting in an old store somewhere, talking about white trucks and green tractors.

CONTENTS

Foreword   6

Acknowledgments   7

Introduction   8

1.   The Battle   11

2.   The Community   29

3.   Monuments and Memorials   43

4.   The Harper House   57

5.   Establishing a Historic Site   81

6.   Programs and Events   95

7.   Bentonville in the 21st Century   113

FOREWORD

I made my first visit to Bentonville Battlefield State Historic Site in 1997, while stationed at Fort Bragg, now identified as Fort Liberty. The battlefield sparked my interest, as I had just completed reading Mark Bradley's excellent Civil War history, *Last Stand in the Carolinas: The Battle of Bentonville*. At that time, the battlefield consisted of only 225 preserved acres out of an estimated 6,000 acres of battlespace—Bentonville proved the largest land battle ever fought in North Carolina during the Civil War. It was while visiting the site that weekend almost three decades ago that I began an equally long journey as a student of Gen. William T. Sherman's 1865 Carolinas Campaign.

I am proud to say that in 2024 the Bentonville battlefield, nestled in rural Johnston County, now consists of more than 2,100 preserved acres, highlighted by miles of walking trails and numerous wayside pullovers, for both current and future generations to study and enjoy. This accomplishment demonstrates the strong love that many of the families that make up the modern-day Bentonville community have for the battlefield. Images of America: *Bentonville Battlefield State Historic Site* wonderfully documents this cooperation between the North Carolina Department of Cultural Resources and the locals.

The coauthors use photographs, maps, and historical documents to tell a story different from the traditional narrative of the battle—a story of the battlefield since 1865 and how it was managed by the community and, later, the state historic site. Although only one original structure from the period remains, the reader of *Bentonville Battlefield* will find the stories passed down from the families that witnessed the great battle and the efforts to preserve the battlefield by the generations that followed, as well as the history of their rural community, a wealth of knowledge.

—Wade Sokolosky
Colonel, US Army (Ret.)
Beaufort, North Carolina

ACKNOWLEDGMENTS

So much gratitude is owed to so many for helping this project come to fruition. First is Chad Jefferds, now of Fort Fisher State Historic Site, for assisting with the early phases of this process. Thanks are also owed to site manager Colby Stevens, Anna Kulcsar, and the entire Bentonville Battlefield family for their aid and patience. That family includes the Friends of Bentonville Battlefield, Inc. Without the support of Donna Bailey-Taylor, Rob Boyette, Dean Harry, Pattie Smith, Wade Sokolosky, and the membership at large, this manuscript wouldn't exist.

It is a Sisyphean task for us to list everyone who helped locate photographs and identified people in them, yet we will attempt to do so anyway. Please know that if anyone we consulted isn't listed it is an error of omission, not commission.

Foremost is Debra Westbrook, who will tell you that she is "not from Bentonville," despite living there since 1980. Debra, through her local contacts and photographic memory for genealogy, was indispensable during this effort. We also relied tremendously on the guidance of previous authors in this series, Andrew Cole, Jim McKee, Pamela Baumgartner, and Todd Johnson, as well as Todd's staff at the Johnston County Heritage Center.

The following people, listed alphabetically, were also generous with their time and knowledge: Morris Bass, Mark Bradley, Amanda Brantley, Erin Brown, Eugene and Jann Brown, Carolyn Cole, Curt Cole, Cornell Cox, Vince Cox, Zelda Dunn, Doug Elwell, Vann Evans, Grady Everett, Jeff Fritzinger, John Goode, Lee Gordon, Jane Grantham, Catherine Harper, David Henkel, Rex Hovey, Elaine Kubich, Larry and Sharon Laboda, Glenn Langston, James Langston, Steven Langston, Wilson and Janet Lee, James Lighthizer, John and Zan Lipscomb, Kathy Robertson, Nelson and Ann Rose, Becky Sawyer, Linda Stine, Kent Thompson, Mary Lynn Thornton, Caroline Waller, Eldridge Westbrook, Doug Williams, Royal Windley, and Mark Woolard. Thanks also goes to Amy Jarvis and the team at Arcadia for approaching us and pushing us in this process.

Abbreviations for repositories whose images are contained within are as follows: Library of Congress (LOC), North Carolina Historic Sites (NCSHS), State Archives of North Carolina (SANC), and the North Carolina Museum of History (NCMOH).

INTRODUCTION

In 1866, a group of Civil War veterans made the nearly 1,700-mile round-trip from Kalamazoo, Michigan, to rural southeastern Johnston County, North Carolina, to visit where their commander, Maj. Willard G. Eaton, had been killed the previous year. They not only found Eaton's grave, they recovered his remains for reinterment in Michigan. This perilous journey across a war-ravaged nation marks one of the first known pilgrimages to Bentonville, the site of the Civil War's most climactic battle in North Carolina. These early visitors are part of a legacy—likely over a million people by now—locals, veterans, descendants, Civil War buffs, students, nature lovers, and curious sightseers who have traversed the woods and fields of Bentonville, hallowed ground that means so much to so many.

Though traversed for millennia by Native Americans, colonial settlers did not arrive in this area of rural Johnston County until the 18th century. By the time of the battle, "Bentonsville," as it was then known, was an established village with a modest business district centered on the naval stores trade—resin, tar, pitch, and turpentine for the shipping industry. However, it was the battle that put the community on the map for all but locals. Bentonville is now a household name amongst professional and amateur Civil War historians, with the latter often erroneously calling it the last battle of the war.

Though not the last, Bentonville was one of the war's last major battles and the decisive engagement of Maj. Gen. William T. Sherman's Carolinas Campaign. Despite this, Bentonville is not well known to those with only cursory knowledge of the war, likely due to news of the battle competing against a virtual panoply of dramatic events in the spring of 1865. Headlines in the *New York Times* about Bentonville were quickly replaced by the capture of Richmond, Gen. Robert E. Lee's surrender at Appomattox, and the assassination of Pres. Abraham Lincoln.

It was easy for Bentonville to get lost in the shuffle of 1865 events because the battle's outcome was not decisive in the near term. Gen. Joseph E. Johnston's 20,000 Confederates were unable to destroy an isolated Union army numbering nearly 30,000 men on March 19, 1865, before Sherman arrived in Bentonville the next day with another 30,000 men. Heavy skirmishing continued on March 20 and 21 before the outnumbered Confederates withdrew, planning to fight another day. Sherman was happy to let them go, knowing that his armies were to be reinforced and resupplied in Goldsboro. Following that, he could likely destroy Johnston's command at a place and time of his choosing.

Because there was no resultant engagement, Bentonville proved to be the first and only full-scale attempt made by Southern forces to oppose Sherman's march north from Georgia through the Carolinas in February and March 1865. With 80,000 soldiers engaged, resulting in 4,133 casualties, Bentonville became North Carolina's largest and bloodiest battle. The importance of Bentonville only became clear in retrospect—a battle defined by what didn't happen. Namely, Sherman's march across the Confederate heartland was allowed to continue unabated, showing the South the futility of continued resistance.

There are so many stories of bravery, tragedy, and triumph associated with the battle that a full listing would never fit in these few pages. Perhaps the most obvious is that a small patchwork Confederate army thrown together in the days and weeks before the battle could and would stand toe-to-toe with Sherman's veterans. With surprise working to even the numerical odds, the Southerners did well during the early phases of the battle before their attacks ran out of steam, as perhaps best illustrated by 20-year-old North Carolina colonel Charles W. Broadfoot's description of the "Last Grand Charge of the Army of Tennessee," written decades later:

> It looked like a picture and at our distance was truly beautiful. Several officers led the charge on horseback across an open field in full view, with colors flying and line of battle in such perfect order as to be able to distinguish the several field officers in proper place. . . . It was gallantly done, but it was painful to see how close their battlefield flags were together, regiments being scarcely larger than companies and division[s] not much larger than a regiment should be.

Broadfoot's account paints a picture of an army in name only. The 6,500 Army of Tennessee soldiers who fought at Bentonville were part of a force that had numbered 70,000 just the previous year.

After the shock of the initial surprise wore off, members of the Union army also performed many heroic deeds on the field. Several US regiments withstood the Confederate onslaught, receiving staggering amounts of casualties. The 13th and 14th Michigan as well as the 16th Illinois recorded at Bentonville their highest single-day casualty figures in the entire war. The latter regiment's official unit history says Bentonville "was the last battle of the war the Sixteenth was engaged in, and it was the most terrible of them all."

Four Medals of Honor, the US military's highest award for bravery, were awarded to soldiers for their actions during the battle. Lt. Allan H. Dougall, a native of Scotland, and Michigan's Cpl. Henry Plant received the honor of defending their respective regimental flags from capture. Plant's fellow Michigander, Cpl. George Clute, received the medal for wrestling a Confederate flag away from an enemy officer. Most remarkable is the story of Pvt. Peter T. Anderson, whose Medal of Honor citation reads, "Entirely unassisted, brought from the field an abandoned piece of artillery and saved the gun from falling into the hands of the enemy."

To say that the battle transformed the Bentonville community is a dramatic understatement. The several families inhabiting the area in 1865 were left to pick up the pieces of their lives with the fields, forests, and shops they relied upon now damaged or destroyed. Several residents, such as the John and Amy Harper family, nursed wounded soldiers well after the battle, while others, such as the Harpers' son John J. and the Willis Cole family, lost their homes entirely.

Life was also suddenly different for Bentonville's formerly enslaved residents, who were now liberated. Many remained in the area, often in the same dwellings they had lived in while enslaved. This was impossible for the people enslaved on the Cole Plantation, as their homes were also destroyed when the Confederates burned the Cole house and buildings to prevent their use by US snipers during the battle. But out of this tragedy came the triumph of Levin Cole (1830–1908), who built one of the first houses by a formerly enslaved individual in Johnston County. Amazingly remnants of the house remain standing on property still owned by Cole's descendants, a testament to Levin's skills as an artisan.

Bentonville's residents continued to farm, attempting to work around the graves and relics that now cluttered their fields. There were no permanent markers for these graves or to indicate there had been a battle at all. This finally changed in 1895 with the erection of the Goldsboro Rifles monument on property donated by John and Amy Harper, erected to mark a Confederate cemetery maintained by the now elderly Harpers. Many veterans of the battle, including keynote speaker Wade Hampton, made the journey to see the marker dedicated. The spotlight was once again on the Bentonville community as news of the monument's March 20, 1895, unveiling populated headlines in state newspapers. This attention was fleeting, however, as the battlefield had to wait over 30 more years for another monument and momentum to permanently preserve the battlefield site.

The North Carolina chapter of the United Daughters of the Confederacy erected Bentonville's second monument in 1927. The monument was accompanied by the battle's first interpretation, a billboard with a map of the battle lines located at the intersection of modern Bass and Harper House Roads. The monument's dedication sparked efforts from multiple prominent North Carolinians, including the state's governor and congressional delegation, for Bentonville's selection as a national battlefield park—efforts that continued into the early 1940s. Any hopes of Bentonville being administered by the federal government in this era were dashed by America's entry into World War II. Congress understandably tabled national park discussions on Bentonville for financial reasons, and these efforts never resumed after the war.

Though detrimental to preservation efforts, World War II proved beneficial to the battlefield in other ways. The war caused the proliferation of military bases in Eastern North Carolina, which brought a new wave of visitation, this time with soldiers interested in the experiences of their forebearers in earlier wars. Soldiers from Fort Liberty, marines and sailors from Camp Lejeune, and airmen from Goldsboro's Seymore Johnson Air Force Base continue to visit the battlefield today, often as part of their training.

It was finally North Carolina that stepped up to permanently preserve a portion of Bentonville in 1957 with the purchase of the Harper House and surrounding property. The c. 1855 house remained in good shape, making restoration to its original appearance possible. Seven years later, a visitor center was built on an adjacent lot just in time for the 100th anniversary of the battle. For 30 more years, the newly christened Bentonville Battleground State Historic Site (later renamed Bentonville Battlefield) consisted primarily of just the Harper House and visitor center. Nearly all the 6,000-acre battlefield remained in private hands, largely owned by the descendants of those who lived in Bentonville in 1865.

The importance of preserving Bentonville finally reached national audiences when it was made a Priority I–Class A battlefield in need of additional preservation by the Congressionally appointed Civil War Sites Advisory Commission in 1993. The commission, which included luminaries such as Dr. James McPherson, Edwin Bearss, and filmmaker Ken Burns, lamented that Bentonville was barely preserved and was in danger of private development. Based upon these recommendations, a partnership was formed between North Carolina and the Civil War Preservation Trust (now American Battlefield Trust), with help from the National Park Service's American Battlefield Protection Program, to purchase additional acreage. As of publication, over 2,000 acres of Bentonville have been preserved, and more than 60,000 people visit Bentonville Battlefield State Historic Site annually.

This publication grew out of the authors' love of Bentonville Battlefield. However, this is not meant to be a retelling of the Battle of Bentonville. For a book-length study of the battle, the authors recommend Dr. Mark L. Bradley's *Last Stand in the Carolinas: The Battle of Bentonville* (published by Savas Woodbury in 1995) and the corresponding map guidebook *Moore's Historical Guide to the Battle of Bentonville* (published by Savas in 1997) by Mark A. Moore. Neither is this project intended to be a history of the Bentonville community and its families except as they relate to the battlefield. The Bentonville community's rich heritage could easily support a book project of its own.

People make the Bentonville story—the families who picked up the pieces of the ravaged landscape, the veterans who first made pilgrimages, the historians who desired to preserve the sites of tragedy and bravery, the descendants connecting to their ancestors, the visitors hoping to learn something new, and the dedicated staff and volunteers who labored to make those experiences possible. It is the authors' fervent desire that these images relay the story of the struggles, victories, and labor that went into the creation of Bentonville Battlefield State Historic Site and making it the place it is today.

One

THE BATTLE

The Battle of Bentonville was the largest fought in North Carolina. Bentonville was the last opportunity for Gen. Joseph Johnston's Confederate army to stop Maj. Gen. William T. Sherman's two US armies or "wings" from reaching Goldsboro, a vital railroad hub. As depicted in this contemporary map, the outnumbered Confederates hoped to even the odds by defeating one Union army before the other could reach the field. (LOC.)

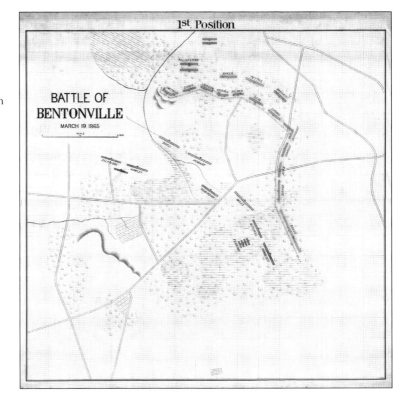

BATTLE OF BENTONSVILLE, NORTH CAROLINA, March 19—FOU

Although no photographs exist of the Battle of Bentonville, drawings like this one provide insight into how it may have appeared. This sketch by William Waud, who personally witnessed the battle, first appeared in *Harper's Weekly* on April 15, 1865. William and his more famous brother Alfred were two of the most prolific sketch artist correspondents of the Civil War. The slow nature of Civil War–era photography meant that it was impractical to capture active battle scenes. However, artists like the Wauds could rapidly draw the outline of a scene and fill in the details before sending it for publication. This particular drawing depicts Union

H AND TWENTIETH CORPS ENGAGED.—[Sketched by W. Waud.]

defenses on the Reddick Morris farm, located on the extreme west end of the battlefield. In the background, entrenched US infantry fire at advancing Confederates, while in the foreground, artillery batteries from the Union 14th and 20th Corps are deployed amongst a stand of longleaf pines. Bentonville's landscape featured sandy farm fields interspersed with these towering trees and overgrown swamps, which were virtually impassable. (Wilson Library, University of North Carolina at Chapel Hill [UNC-Chapel Hill].)

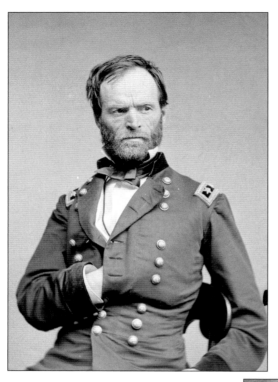

As commander of the Military Division of the Mississippi, Maj. Gen. William Tecumseh Sherman commanded all Union armies between the Carolinas and the Mississippi River. He personally oversaw operations during the 1865 Carolinas Campaign and during the second and third days of the Battle of Bentonville. The two armies under Sherman's immediate command totaled nearly 60,000 men. (LOC.)

A reluctant Gen. Joseph Eggleston Johnston came out of retirement to oppose Sherman in February 1865 at the request of Gen. Robert E. Lee. At Bentonville, Johnston's newly constituted Army of the South was approximately 20,000 strong and consisted of elements of the Army of Tennessee, the Department of North Carolina, the Department of South Carolina, Georgia, and Florida, and Wade Hampton's cavalry command. (National Archives.)

To develop a sense of camaraderie, each corps in the Union army had its own emblem, akin to a modern-day logo. Soldiers often wore the emblem somewhere on their uniforms. The four corps engaged at Bentonville were the 14th, 15th, 17th, and 20th. Depicted here surrounding an image of Sherman, their badges were an acorn, a cartridge box with "40 rounds" emblazoned on it, an arrow, and a star, respectively. (LOC.)

These brass acorn artifacts, worn by soldiers in the 14th Corps, were recovered from the battlefield. Competing origin stories have the acorn chosen because the men "stood like oak" at Chickamauga or that they survived by eating acorns during an early-war campaign. Soldiers from the 20th Corps began calling Bentonville the "Battle of Acorn Run," derisively named due to the hasty retreat of one 14th Corps division. (NCSHS.)

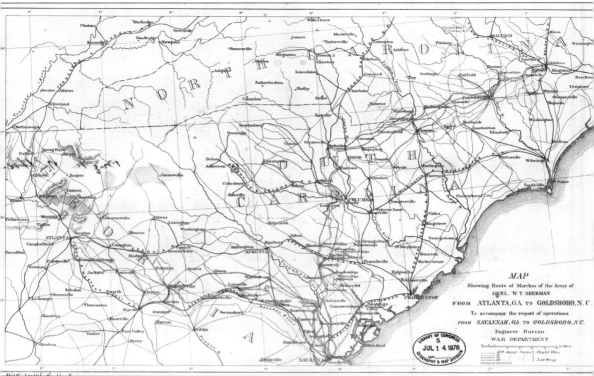

MAP
Showing Route of Marches of the Army of
GEN^{l}. W.T. SHERMAN
FROM ATLANTA, GA. TO GOLDSBORO, N.C.
To accompany the report of operations
FROM SAVANNAH, GA. TO GOLDSBORO, N.C.
Engineer Bureau
WAR DEPARTMENT

The route of US forces through Georgia and the subsequent Carolinas Campaign is illustrated on this contemporary map prepared by army engineers to accompany Sherman's after-action report. Although difficult to see, the five lines show the roads that the four corps and the cavalry took through the region. While still in Georgia, Sherman had one eye on Goldsboro, North Carolina, as his destination for the march. The town may not seem like a strategic locale today, but Sherman valued Goldsboro due to railroads that went east and south to port cities under—or soon to be under—US control. Repairing the railroad would allow for the resupply of Sherman's command, which had previously been isolated in Confederate territory. Reinforcements were also scheduled to meet Sherman in Eastern North Carolina. The bulk of Sherman's command crossed from Georgia to South Carolina during the first days of February 1865 and arrived in Goldsboro by March 24. The 20th Corps reported covering 465 miles on foot during this period. (LOC.)

Sherman and several of his general officers are shown in this May 1865 image (above) taken at Mathew Brady's Washington, DC, studio during the Grand Review of the Union armies at the close of the war. From left to right are (seated) Maj. Gen. James Logan, Sherman, and Maj. Gen. Henry Slocum; (standing) Maj. Gen. O.O. Howard, Maj. Gen. William Hazen, Maj. Gen. Jefferson Davis, and Maj. Gen. Joseph Mower. Absent from the above image is Maj. Gen. Francis Blair Jr. Blair was late arriving for the scheduled session, so the photograph was taken without him. When Blair finally arrived, he was photographed separately and added to later versions (below) of the image—today's photoshopping. (Both, LOC.)

The mercurial Gen. Braxton Bragg commanded the Department of North Carolina, which comprised almost half of Johnston's Confederate army at Bentonville. Bragg was an unpopular figure who was disliked by nearly everyone. He did have at least one powerful ally in Confederate president Jefferson Davis. Johnston detested Bragg (largely due to his ties to Davis) but made a point of shelving his animosity to set a positive example for the army. (LOC.)

Lt. Gen. William. J. Hardee, "Old Reliable," commanded the other half of Johnston's Confederate army at Bentonville. Hardee's Corps, tasked with the unenviable job of buying time for Johnston to concentrate his forces, engaged the Union Left Wing at the Battle of Averasboro on March 16. At Bentonville on March 19, Hardee's command was ordered to charge the Left Wing as it deployed to dislodge Bragg, whose force blocked the Goldsboro Road. (LOC.)

It was not a surprise to Confederate officers like Lt. Gen. Wade Hampton III that Sherman was likely headed toward Goldsboro once he moved into Eastern North Carolina. Hampton was Johnston's capable cavalry commander, feeding his superior information about Sherman's movements while also helping to conceal Confederate intentions. It was Hampton who discovered that Bentonville was a great place for Johnston to ambush the Left Wing before it reached Goldsboro. (LOC.)

Of his cavalry commander, H. Judson Kilpatrick, Sherman wrote, "I know that Kilpatrick is a hell of a damned fool, but I want just that sort of man to command my cavalry on this expedition." "Little Kil" incorrectly told Sherman that Johnston's army was falling back toward Raleigh after the fight at Averasboro instead of making a stand outside of Goldsboro. (LOC.)

Brig. Gen. William P. Carlin commanded the 14th Corps' First Division. In 1889, Carlin professed to have known on March 18 that there would be a battle the following day. Carlin claimed this foreknowledge inspired him to wear his finest uniform. It is equally plausible that Carlin wanted to be well dressed when his division reached the Goldsboro outskirts. Either way, his impulsiveness spelled disaster for his command at Bentonville. (Smithsonian Institution.)

Brig. Gen. James D. Morgan was the anti-Carlin. As commander of the 14th Corps' Second Division, Morgan was unimaginative but reliable. Despite being surrounded by Confederates on three sides and an impassable swamp on the fourth—an area dubbed "the bullpen" by the encircled soldiers—most of Morgan's division held its position when Carlin's troops ran. Morgan's stand was the beginning of the end of Confederate successes on March 19. (Abraham Lincoln Presidential Library and Museum.)

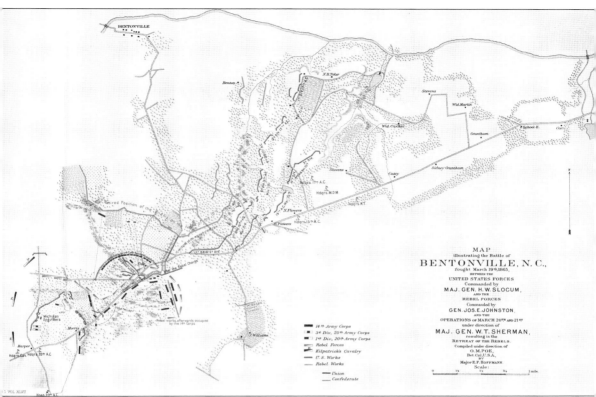

MAP
illustrating the Battle of
BENTONVILLE, N.C.,
fought March 19th,1865,
BETWEEN THE
UNITED STATES FORCES
Commanded by
MAJ. GEN. H.W. SLOCUM,
AND THE
REBEL FORCES
Commanded by
GEN. JOS. E. JOHNSTON,
AND THE
OPERATIONS OF MARCH 20TH AND 21ST
under direction of
MAJ. GEN. W.T. SHERMAN,
resulting in the
RETREAT OF THE REBELS.
Compiled under direction of
O. M. POE,
Bvt. Col. U.S.A.,
BY
Major E. F. Hoffmann.
Scale :

▬▬▬	14th Army Corps	
▬▬▬	3d Div, 20th Army Corps	
▬▬▬	1st Div, 20th Army Corps	
▬▬▬	Rebel Forces	
▬▬▬	Kilpatrick's Cavalry	
▬▬▬	U. S. Works	
▬▬▬	Rebel Works	
——	Union	
——	Confederate	

Engineers Col. Orlando Poe and Maj. Ernest Hoffman compiled this map published in the 1890s to supplement the *War of the Rebellion* series. The first day's fight between Johnston's army and the Left Wing is depicted on the left side of the map. The arrival of the Right Wing and the subsequent Confederate redeployment is shown on the right. Despite Johnston's inability to defeat the Left Wing, he surprisingly chose to remain on the field and risk facing Sherman's entire command. Knowing he was drastically outnumbered, Johnston tried to create strong defensive works on the south side of Mill Creek, hoping Sherman would attack him—an extremely risky plan for the Confederates, whose backs were against the rain-swollen creek. Perhaps fortuitously for the Southerners, Sherman was reluctant to continue that battle unless forced. (Wilson Library, UNC–Chapel Hill.)

The vulnerable nature of the Confederates' position along Mill Creek was exposed by a surprise assault on March 21 by Maj. Gen. Joseph Mower's 17th Corps. Accompanying Mower was William Waud, who drew this sketch of "Mower's Charge." Johnston himself was nearly captured, and had Mower been supported, the entire Confederate army may have been captured. Instead, Sherman was angry that Mower attacked without permission and withheld reinforcements. (Wilson Library, UNC–Chapel Hill.)

The Confederate escape on the night of March 21 allowed the Civil War to continue in North Carolina. Sherman proceeded to Goldsboro, where his armies were resupplied and reinforced. He set out in pursuit of Johnston's army on April 9 and eventually accepted Johnston's final surrender on April 26 at the Bennett farm in present-day Durham. William Waud provided this sketch of Sherman and Johnston's meeting to *Harper's Weekly*. (NCSHS.)

Junior officers from the 105th Ohio pose in this 1863 image. Their uniforms were typical of the soldiers in Sherman's command at the beginning of the campaign. By the time they reached Bentonville, many wore civilian attire they had confiscated along the way to replace their tattered uniforms. Lt. Albion Tourgee, on the left, later represented Homer Plessy in the notorious *Plessy v. Ferguson* trial in 1896. (Chautauqua County Historical Society.)

Officers from the 57th Georgia and their cook Scott (center right), who was likely enslaved by Capt. J.R. Bonner (center left), posed for this photograph during the war. Their uniforms were typical of the Army of Tennessee, which made up a quarter of Johnston's Bentonville army. Joining Bonner and Scott are Lt. Archibald McKinley (left) and Lt. William Stetson (right). Stetson was wounded at Bentonville by an artillery fragment. (Georgia College & State University.)

Marching at the head of the 13th Michigan, Col. Willard Eaton (left) was shot through the forehead early in the afternoon of March 19 on the Cole Plantation, killing him immediately. Two days later, a burial detail found Eaton "stripped of all but underclothes" with seven others in a shallow grave that had been dug by Confederates. They fashioned a makeshift grave marker out of an ammunition chest lid (below) to mark the site where they reburied him. A year later, Eaton's body was reinterred in his hometown of Otsego, Michigan, by veterans of the 13th Michigan. (Both, Otsego Area Historical Museum.)

First Lt. Henry A. Watson, Company F, 16th Regiment, Illinois Infantry, posed for this photograph prior to the Carolinas Campaign. On March 20th, a miscommunication between Watson's regimental commander and the colonel of the 14th Michigan led to a disastrous charge in which the Illinoisians lost one-third of their regiment to Confederate artillery and musket fire. Watson was one of those wounded during the assault. (LOC.)

Capt. John W. Taylor from neighboring Sampson County led a company of North Carolina artillerymen fighting as infantry in an assault on Morgan's position in the bullpen. Taylor was shot through the spine while rallying his men. The paralyzed captain lingered for two weeks before succumbing to his wounds at a Raleigh hospital. Two of his brothers also became Bentonville casualties. This funeral notice includes a lock of Taylor's hair. (Michael Y. Taylor.)

FUNERAL NOTICE.

The Funeral of Capt. JOHN W. TAYLOR, of New Hanover County, 1st Battalion Artillery N. C. T., will take place from the Baptist Church this afternoon at 4 o'clock.

The friends and acquaintances of the deceased are invited to be present.

Tuesday, April 4th, 1865.

Lock of his hair.

Teenage North Carolina Military Academy cadet John H. Curtis (left) withdrew from school in 1862 to enlist as an artillerist. Between battles, Curtis sent a constant stream of often humorous letters to his sister. In one letter (below), written on captured Union stationery, he teases her for not yet being wed at 17: "I hope you won't begin to feel too much like an old woman . . . you mustn't give up all hope." At a relatively quiet time on March 21 at Bentonville, Curtis was shot through the head, killing him instantly. His final letter had closed forebodingly with "times look dark. We can hope for better, keeping our trust in Him and to ourselves. May he grant us a speedy and glorious deliverance from the troubles now threatening us." (Both, NCSHS.)

One of the Battle of Bentonville's more unique participants was Lucy Higgs Nichols (standing center), photographed here at an 1898 reunion of the 23rd Indiana Regiment. Born enslaved in 1838 in Halifax County, North Carolina, Nichols was in Tennessee with her enslavers in 1862 when she chose the opportunity of a Union offensive to self-emancipate, escaping with her three-year-old daughter Mona to Union lines. In exchange for the protection they provided against re-enslavement, a grateful Lucy decided to remain with the 23rd Indiana as a cook, laundress, and nurse. Lucy was often in harm's way as she attended to the wounded of the regiment that were engaged as part of Sherman's Right Wing at Bentonville. After the war, Lucy became an honorary member of the Grand Army of the Republic, a fraternal organization of Union veterans of the Civil War. Finally, in 1898, after much lobbying by Lucy and veterans of the 23rd, a literal act of Congress was passed granting her a Federal pension. She died in 1915 in New Albany, Indiana. (Floyd County Library.)

This Medal of Honor—the US military's highest commendation for valor—was awarded to the 14th Michigan's Henry E. Plant by Congress in 1896 for protecting his regiment's flag from capture during the March 19, 1865, fight for the bullpen at Bentonville. Medals of Honor were also awarded in 1897 to Lt. Allan H. Dougall for saving the 88th Indiana's flag on the Cole Plantation and to Plant's fellow Michigander Cpl. George Clute in 1898 for capturing the 40th North Carolina flag, also during the bullpen fight. The 1890s saw Congress issue many of these ex-post-facto Medals of Honor when it received corroborating evidence that one was deserved. In some cases, the applicants could supply this evidence themselves if there were no witnesses. Bentonville's only Medal of Honor issued in the battle's immediate aftermath was awarded to Wisconsin's Peter T. Anderson, who single-handedly saved a US cannon from falling into Confederate hands. (Candace Busman.)

Two

THE COMMUNITY

Bentonville seemed an unlikely place for a battle when Confederate chief engineer Maj. Gen. Jeremy Gilmer ordered his staff to create this map early in the Civil War. Gilmer had the foresight to appreciate Bentonville's strategic importance due to the many crossroads nearby, thus prompting the map's creation. The farms of prominent landowners John Harper, Reddick Morris, Willis Cole, and Green Flowers appear near the bottom of the map. (Wilson Library, UNC-Chapel Hill.)

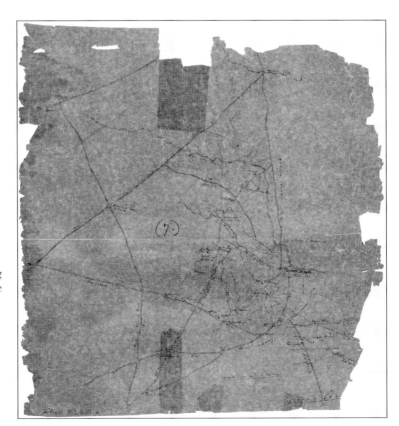

VIEW OF BENTONVILLE, N. C, THE MORNING AFTER THE BATTLE GREAT QUA

This sketch shows the small village of Bentonville on Wednesday, March 22, 1865, the morning after the battle's end. Though modest in size, Bentonville was a thriving village prior to the battle, featuring several businesses including a carriage shop and a turpentine distillery, industries extremely susceptible to fire. Bentonville's economy mostly revolved around farming and the distillation and transportation of turpentine, made from the longleaf pine trees that proliferated

ROSIN FIRED BY THE REBELS.—FROM A SKETCH BY OUR SPECIAL ARTIST

in the area. Following the battle, most of the village of Bentonville had burned, either due to spreading fires from the battle or by soldiers' torches. This William Waud sketch for *Harper's Weekly* shows the village burning in the background with Union soldiers standing near freshly dug graves in the foreground. Little of Bentonville's business district remained after the fires finally burned themselves out, and the village never truly recovered from the battle. (SANC.)

THE TURPENTINE INDUSTRY IN NORTH CAROLINA.—Drawn by W. P. Snyder.—[See Page 325.]

Unlike its neighbors north and south, the Tar Heel State's agrarian economy wasn't chained to traditional cash crop staples tobacco and cotton. In the antebellum era, turpentine orchards were more common in Eastern North Carolina and Bentonville than cotton fields. The Atlantic Coastal Plain's sandy fields were the perfect breeding ground for the longleaf pine (*Pinus palustris*), a tree earmarked during the colonial period for its value in the burgeoning naval stores trade. Naval stores included tar, pitch, and turpentine, vital components in the shipbuilding process, with many other far-reaching applications. Creating these substances required the pine's sap, which was released by etching a "cat's face" into a tree by carving slits resembling whiskers. This 1884 sketch from *Harper's Weekly* depicts the turpentine process, including extracting sap, turpentine distillation, storage, and shipping. Before the Civil War, both free and enslaved workers toiled in the extremely labor-intensive trade. The overharvesting of longleaf pines ended the trade in North Carolina before the turn of the 20th century. (SANC.)

The Harper, Morris, and Cole farms all harvested sap for processing at a large turpentine distillery in the village prior to the end of the naval stores industry in Bentonville. Bentonville's naval stores legacy remains visible in this pine stump photographed in 1957. Note the deep V indented into the tree, remnants of the "cat face" etched into the tree to channel the sap for easier collection. (NCMOH.)

Alonzo "Lon" Thornton (cut off at the top of the photograph) and his family break from their work in a cotton field to pose for this early-20th-century photograph. The end of the naval stores industry in Bentonville meant a transition to extensive cotton and tobacco farming. Lon's family lived just south of the Harper Farm, which was purchased by his father, Samuel Isaac Thornton, in 1903. (Mary Lynn Thornton.)

Already considered old by some at the time of the battle, the Stevens House (above) was in poor condition when photographed in 1957. The "wine and brandy house" and adjacent wagon shed (below) on the property were in better shape but still dilapidated. In 1934, the *Charlotte Observer* noted that these structures showed scars from the battle—surprisingly so considering the home's location on the extreme eastern edge of the battlefield. Lore states that these buildings were used as a battlefield hospital, but this has not been corroborated by historical records. Unless briefly used as a temporary aid station, the house's location made it unsuitable for medical use by either army. During the battle, the property was likely owned by John Stevens Sr. (1834–1903). (Both, NCMOH.)

Levin (or Leven) Cole (1836–1908) built this house between 1870 and 1880, making it the earliest surviving dwelling in Johnston County constructed by a formerly enslaved person. Levin and wife Harriet (Morris) raised seven children in the home. The building was vacated by 1980, when this photograph was taken. The house remains standing on property owned by descendants of Levin. (Thomas R. Butchko, Johnston County Architectural Survey.)

The Old Cole Cemetery, located behind Levin's home, has marked graves dating back to 1906. Leven himself was interred here in 1908, followed by his wife, Harriet Morris Cole, in 1921. Other graves of note in the cemetery include Levin's relative Hinton Cole Monk and his wife, Sarah Williams Monk. The Monks were the grandparents of jazz legend Thelonious S. Monk. (Authors' collection.)

This photograph of the Eldridge T. Westbrook House was taken around 1910. Westbrook's wife, Geneva E. (Woodall) Westbrook, is standing on the left with several of their children. Eldridge himself may be seated on the porch. This 1890s structure is another example of postwar construction in Bentonville. Identical homes were built by the Westbrooks' relatives in nearby Sampson County. (Johnston County Heritage Center.)

The Micajah and Mehettebell Jinett Cox family of Bentonville posed for this photograph in the 1890s. Micajah was born into a Quaker family in 1847 in nearby Wayne County. The house in this picture was located near the present-day intersection of Harper House Road and US Highway 701. The Cox and Westbrook families were linked through marriage in the early 20th century. (Johnston County Heritage Center.)

The oldest remaining house of worship in Bentonville, the original Bentonville Disciples of Christ Church building is shown in this recent photograph. The congregation was founded in 1866 by local residents, many of whom were born into slavery. A modern church has been built on the property, and this building is still used for special events and historic preservation. (Authors' collection.)

Brothers Worth (left) and Tim (center) Westbrook with cousin Gary Langston pose in front of Ebenezer United Methodist Church in the early 1960s. The land for Ebenezer Church was deeded by C.M. Cogdell in 1895. The original one-room church stands within the structure seen here, which is still in use. Ebenezer is located at Flowers' Crossroads, where Confederate cavalry clashed with Sherman's Right Wing on March 20. (Debra Westbrook.)

Mill Creek Church's origins date to 1793, when the then-Baptist congregation began meeting in a small log structure. Following Mill Creek's conversion to the new Disciples of Christ denomination in 1845, John Harper donated land on the northern edge of his property for an improved church building and a public school, one of the first in the county. The new two-story church (above) was located on the west side of the road leading north from Harper's home. The school (below) was constructed across the road. The modern Mill Creek Church, built in the 1930s, stands where the school once was. The old building site became the church cemetery. (Above, Debra Westbrook; below, Johnston County Heritage Center.)

St. John Pentecostal Holiness Church is located near the heart of modern Bentonville, close to the intersection of Devil's Racetrack and Harper House Roads. Like neighboring Ebenezer Church, St. John was founded toward the end of the 19th century on land that had seen heavy fighting during the battle's second day. (Authors' collection.)

St. John Church member Facie Thornton (1906–1984) is seen here with his log truck. The evaporation of the naval stores trade meant that local trees would now be targeted for timber instead of sap. Second only to agriculture, the lumber industry was vital for Bentonville's economy during the 20th century. (Mary Lynn Thornton.)

Roadside wells were commonly seen in rural areas such as Bentonville, allowing passing travelers access to fresh water in the days before convenience stores. This 1957 image shows one of these roadside wells that sat near the current location of the visitor center. The newly constructed Dunn residence can be seen on the right side of the photograph. A pump house now sits where the well once stood. (SANC.)

Built in 1940, C.W. Flowers' is Bentonville's only retail outlet. If someone's tractor needs a tire, Flowers' has it. If they forget something on their grocery list, Flowers' has that too. More importantly, the store serves as a gathering place for the community, where locals congregate to solve Bentonville's and the world's problems. Then owner and later co-owner Wilson Lee poses outside the store in this 1980s image. (Wilson and Janet Lee.)

Across the road from Flowers' stands the Bentonville Volunteer Fire Department. Like the store, the fire department is another pillar of the community, with many of Bentonville's residents having some affiliation with the department. This 1985 image shows members, from left to right, Buck Dunn, Ricky Jackson, Eldridge Westbrook, James Beasley, Wilson Lee, Andy Lee, and Tim Westbrook in front of the new firehouse. (Johnston County Heritage Center.)

Bentonville's namesake, John Benton (1794–1875), owned a plantation a half-mile east of Mill Creek Bridge. In his 1872 will, the lifelong bachelor requested a brick tomb for his grave. Allegedly an estranged sweetheart had threatened to "eat the goose that eats the grass off of his grave," leading to Benton requesting the bricks. In 2004, Matthew Creech restored Benton's gravesite for his Eagle Scout project, this time without bricks. (Author's collection.)

It is difficult to spot any semblance of Bentonville's 19th-century business district in this pair of photographs taken on the eve of the battle's 125th anniversary. The Bentonville community building (above) stands as a place for locals to meet and as a polling place during elections. Land for this building was donated in 1950 by the Beasley family, and the building seen here was built shortly thereafter. It is likely that the William Waud sketch on the second and third pages of this chapter was drawn standing near this building's location looking north toward Mill Creek Bridge. In the image below, the community building stands in the background as the viewer faces south on Devil's Racetrack Road. Sadly, to the authors' knowledge, no pre–Civil War buildings remain standing in what was once a high-commerce area. (Both, Johnston County Heritage Center.)

Three

MONUMENTS AND MEMORIALS

The first permanent monument to the battle was erected by the Goldsboro Rifles, a North Carolina State Guard unit from neighboring Wayne County, on property donated by John Harper. Work began on the monument in 1894, and it was officially unveiled on March 20, 1895. The wooden head and foot markers in the background indicate Confederate graves reinterred to this location. (SANC.)

Former Confederate cavalry chief and retired US senator Wade Hampton (left) was the keynote speaker at the Goldsboro Rifles' monument dedication. As a gifted orator and strong proponent of the "Lost Cause," Hampton was often requested to speak at monument dedications such as the one in Bentonville. His presence provided some symmetry, however, as Hampton personally chose Bentonville as the place for Johnston to make his stand in March 1865. Hampton stayed on the Harper farm in 1865 and then again for the dedication in 1895. Event organizers expected thousands to attend the ceremony, but torrential rains limited attendance to a few hundred people, including these folks (below) posing outside of a building purported to be the dwelling for the enslaved on the Harper farm. Considering slavery had ended three decades before, this structure could also be a simple outbuilding (Left, LOC; below, SANC.)

This photograph (above) was taken on March 20, 1895, dedication day for the Goldsboro Rifles monument on the Harper farm, because the couple are both wearing badges sold to raise funds for the monument. Long thought to be John and Amy Harper, recent research has pointed toward this being one of the Harpers' children and their spouse. It is possible the image was captured on the Harper farm, but this structure is shaped differently than the Harper House. The couple are wearing this badge (right), which features the outline of the monument and the words "Goldsboro Rifles Confederate Monument, Unveiling Mar. 20, 1895," with "Bentonsville, N.C.," across the top. (Above, SANC; right, NCSHS.)

The Goldsboro Rifles monument at Bentonville was just one in a series of memorials that proliferated throughout the South in the 1890s. This postcard from 1897 shows Capt. T.H. Bain, commander of the Goldsboro Rifles, viewing the monument. The following year, Bain and his men were deployed to Cuba during the Spanish-American War. A rail fence separates the Confederate and Harper cemeteries from the fields on the Harper farm. (NCSHS.)

Veterans and their families visited Bentonville in the decades following the battle. Some features of the landscape, such as this tree photographed in 1897, still bore the scars of the fighting that occurred in 1865 and drew much attention from visitors and returning veterans, becoming a testament and memorial to the events that happened there. (NCSHS.)

This early-20th-century image of the Goldsboro Rifles monument was taken from the east side of the marker. Each side of the monument lists several Confederate soldiers, most of whom died in the battle, and says that "about 360 unknown Confederate dead are buried here." The monument also mentions the contributions of the Harper family, whose former house and farmstead can be seen in the background. (NCMOH.)

Erected by the United Daughters of the Confederacy and the North Carolina Historical Commission in 1927, the second monument on the battlefield honored the North Carolina Junior Reserves who fought at Bentonville. These teenage Tar Heels were stationed near the center of the Confederate line throughout the battle. Their monument was erected close to their position on the battle's first day. (NCSHS.)

In 1927, Fred Olds, dressed in a safari hat and long jacket (standing, right), gave a tour of Bentonville Battlefield to three unidentified people, photographed here with the Junior Reserves monument (above) and a large map of the battle. Perhaps North Carolina's most active historian during the early 20th century, the artifacts and knowledge Olds collected formed the basis of the North Carolina Hall of History, later renamed the Museum of History. Olds spoke often of the Junior Reserves battalion, or "Boys' Brigade," and was instrumental in researching the battle and selecting the spot for the monument. Olds's party also toured some of the remaining breastworks (below) on the battlefield. Miles of original earthworks remain on the battlefield in the 21st century. When visiting Bentonville today, please do not follow Olds's example and climb on the trenches. (Both, NCMOH.)

On the eve of the Great Depression, a survey placed the battlefield at Bentonville in class 2A for possible selection as a national park. These two monuments on different areas of the battleground were photographed in 1934, the same year the *News and Observer* advertised that a historian from the Department of Interior would be inspecting the site for its suitability as a national park. At right, the 1895 Goldsboro Rifles monument is overgrown. Below, the Junior Reserves monument is adorned with greenery. Ralston Lattimore from the National Park Service (NPS) did indeed conduct a feasibility study that December. His recommendation that Bentonville should become a national park went unheeded. (Both, NCMOH.)

On May 13, 1934, the state chapter of the United Daughters of the Confederacy (UDC) organized a Confederate Memorial Day event on the front lawn of the Harper House. Speakers Lucy London Woodard, president of the state chapter of the UDC, and Congressional candidate George Ross Pou, second from left above, introduced keynote speaker Judge Henry Stevens, former national commander of the American Legion, pictured fourth from left above. Speakers at the event voiced the need to preserve Bentonville as a national park and discussed their plans to make that a reality. Below, visitors gather around their cars in the oak grove in front of the Harper House for the event. (Both, NCMOH.)

Between the Depression and the onset of World War II, funding for a national park never materialized. Instead, the Battle of Bentonville was interpreted elsewhere, such as at Raleigh's Hall of History, the precursor of the North Carolina Museum of History. This photograph, taken in the museum, shows two projectile-riddled Civil War artifacts on display: the funnel of the CSS *Albemarle* (right) and a tree from Bentonville (left). (NCMOH.)

Despite the failure of early preservation efforts, few other Civil War battlefields could boast of the miles of trenches that still remained in Bentonville into the mid-20th century. Raleigh's *News and Observer* in 1934 had described Bentonville's well-preserved breastworks and war-scarred grounds as the "best preserved important battle site in the country." This picture was taken during a photographic survey of Bentonville's earthworks in the 1950s. (SANC.)

In these 1940s-era photographs, local young people gather around Bentonville monuments, which seems appropriate considering they grew up living on or near a battlefield. Above, from left to right, Seth Westbrook, Mildred Westbrook Langston, Edna Westbrook, and Leon George Westbrook Jr. pose on the Goldsboro Rifles monument during the mid-1940s. At left, Kathleen Thornton Britt and Henry Britt pose for a photograph in front of the Junior Reserves monument on the battlefield during the same time frame. Army soldiers Seth and Leon Westbrook and Navy seaman Henry Britt all served during World War II. In later years, Mildred Langston became a champion of preserving and interpreting Bentonville Battlefield. (Above, Debra Westbrook; left, Mary Lynn Thornton.)

When the Goldsboro Rifles monument was erected in 1895, Rifles members and the local community maintained the area around the monument. After that generation passed, the monument and cemetery were allowed to fall into disrepair, as shown in this mid-20th-century photograph. In 1956, several papers across North Carolina, including Durham's *Morning Herald* and Rocky Mount's *Telegram*, printed a story referring to Bentonville as an obscure battlefield, referring to it as the least disturbed and least cared-for battlefield in the country. Interest in the Civil War grew in the 1950s, and the rediscovery of this "obscure" battlefield drew attention, which eventually led to the establishment of Bentonville Battleground (later Battlefield) State Historic Site in 1957. After that date, monument upkeep became the responsibility of site staff, as shown in this 1978 photograph below. (Both, SANC.)

In the late 1950s, site staff employed a motor grader to smooth the rough ground between the Harper cemetery and Goldsboro Rifles monument. According to then–site administrator Nicholas Bragg, they had no idea they were plowing over a likely Confederate cemetery. Maintenance worker Jack Rose can be seen in the background cleaning around the Harper graves. Rose later became the site manager. (NCSHS.)

The landscaped monument area can be seen in this 1970s aerial image. The 1895 obelisk is at the bottom of the image, separated by pines from the Harper cemetery, which is near the center. The visitor center driveway is on the far left, while replica field fortifications can be seen on the far right. The grave markers to the left of the monument are Dunn family members. (NCSHS.)

Additional monuments began to proliferate at Bentonville during the second half of the 20th century. The first addition was this pink granite monument placed by the Texas Civil War Centennial Commission at Bentonville in March 1965, the centennial of the battle. Keynote speakers during the presentation were Texas senator Ralph Yarborough and North Carolina senators B. Everett Jordan and Sam J. Ervin Jr. (Authors' collection.)

In 1992, the Harper House–Bentonville Chapter of the United Daughters of the Confederacy erected this monument honoring North Carolina soldiers who fought and died during the Battle of Bentonville. Located near the 1895 Goldsboro Rifles monument and the 1965 Texas monument (both in the background), this addition established what is now known as the "monument area." (NCSHS.)

Beginning in 2007, archaeological surveys near the Goldsboro Rifles monument proved the existence of multiple individual graves—at least 20—but no evidence of a mass grave. While research continues, site staff believe that these are the remains of unknown Confederate soldiers who died in the Harper House after the battle. In 2011, the Harper House–Bentonville Chapter of the UDC purchased tombstones to mark these graves, which can be seen behind the monument. (Donny Taylor.)

When a Union monument was proposed for Bentonville in the 1990s, one prominent state official stated, "Not on my watch," and threatened to retaliate against the site's budget if the monument was built. Finally in 2013, nearly 20 years after the initial efforts began, new state representatives, community members, and veterans' descendants (including the Sons of Union Veterans) brought to fruition a monument honoring Bentonville's US soldiers. (Authors' collection.)

Four

THE HARPER HOUSE

Built in 1855, the Harper House became one of the most iconic structures in Johnston County after its use as a field hospital during the Battle of Bentonville. The owners John and Amy Harper stand on the porch in this 1895 photograph, taken at the dedication of the Goldsboro Rifles monument. Flying from the balcony is a Red Cross flag, indicating the house's earlier use as a hospital. (SANC.)

The Harper Residence. Bentonville N.C. used as Confederate Hospital during and after the battle. Mar. 19, 2

The US Army Medical Corps during the Civil War employed a surgeon and assistant surgeon for each regiment, as well as surgeons and staff for each brigade, division, corps, and army. Henry Appleton Goodale (left, standing far left) had attended medical college and practiced medicine before he was commissioned into the 21st Michigan Infantry as assistant surgeon in 1863. Henry was one of several surgeons who operated on wounded soldiers at the Harper House, working late into the night on March 19 and most of the following two days. The most experienced surgeons conducted the most complicated surgeries, often using an amputation surgical kit like the one below. Contrary to popular belief, 95 percent of all surgeries in the Civil War utilized anesthesia; at Bentonville, surgeons used chloroform to anesthetize patients. (Left, Michigan State University Archives and Historical Collections; below, NCSHS.)

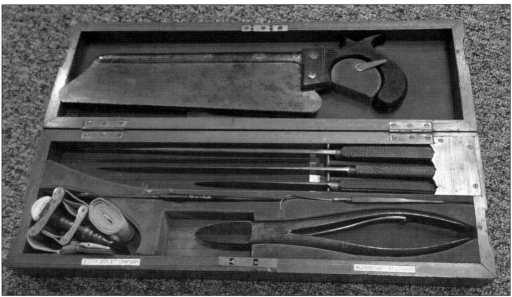

Marcus Bates was shot through the hip on March 19, with the bullet lodging in his scrotum—a wound Surgeon Goodale thought fatal. While resting at the Harper House, Marcus vowed to not fill a North Carolina grave. He survived long enough to be brought to DeCamp General Hospital in New York, where surgeons finally removed the bullet. Bates returned to Michigan, where he remarkably fathered children and lived until 1916. (Mark Krausz.)

A year following his enlistment, 34-year-old Pvt. William Noah was severely wounded on the battle's first day, leading to the amputation of his right arm at the Harper House. Noah recovered swiftly and returned home to Sidney Township, Michigan, to reunite with his wife and five children. After the war, he fathered two more children, served in town politics, and farmed until his death in 1929 at the age of 97. (LOC.)

Amy Ann Harper (1820–1900) married John Harper at the age of 17. Amy's parents, John and Amy Ann Woodard, were prominent farmers in nearby Sampson County. While her home was used as a field hospital, the family remained upstairs, staying out of harm's way. Following the battle, Amy and her family served as nurses, caring for the several Confederate wounded that were treated and left behind by US surgeons. (SANC.)

John Harper (1803–1897) inherited several hundred acres of land in 1841, three years after marrying Amy Ann Woodard. His father, Revolutionary War veteran John Harper Sr. (1762–1834), settled in the Bentonville area in the first decade of the 1800s with his wife Anna Covington (1770–1841), the couple having moved from western Virginia. The elder Harper's uncle Robert was allegedly the namesake of Harpers Ferry. (SANC.)

The Harpers moved from their house in 1897 due to their advanced age and poor health; this photograph was likely taken the day they left the house for the last time. John and Amy spent their final days in Dunn, alternating between the residences of their daughter Martha Hood and son Martin. At 94 years old, John died later that year, and Amy died at the age of 79 in 1900. (NCSHS.)

This c. 1895 photograph shows one of the multiple outbuildings that existed on the Harper farm (far left). Although this structure's usage is unclear, outbuildings were used for kitchens, storehouses, smokehouses, corn cribs, barns, and more. Census data also shows the Harpers owned one dwelling for the enslaved on their farm before the Civil War. Such a structure would have been repurposed by the Harpers after emancipation. (SANC.)

Rev. John J. Harper (1841–1908), the Harpers' oldest son, lived in the village of Bentonville with his wife, Aritta (Daniels). During the battle, their home housed wounded soldiers from both armies before burning in the fire that claimed most of Bentonville. Reverend Harper later represented Johnston County in the state legislature before becoming one of the founders and second president of Atlantic Christian (now Barton) College. (Johnston County Heritage Center.)

Martha, John and Amy Harper's third child, married Rev. Nathan Hood in 1871. The couple are shown here in a c. 1890s portrait. In 1886, the Hoods moved from Bentonville to Dunn, where Nathan built a Disciples of Christ church for which he was the pastor. One of the church's cofounders was Dr. Martin Harper, Martha's brother. The church was later renamed Hood Memorial Church in their honor. (Hood Memorial Christian Church.)

The Harper family cemetery is located a few hundred yards from the Harper House. Those buried there include John and Amy Harper, along with their children Caroline Barbour, Jasper, Marion, and Paschal. John's parents and several grandchildren are also buried there. (SANC.)

Renters occupied the Harper House after John and Amy vacated the property. Following Amy's death, the house was sold in 1903—the year this photograph was taken—to the William T. and Emma (Johnson) Surles family. Later that year, the house was sold a second time to Samuel I. Thornton at a substantial loss for the Surles family, allegedly due to Emma being uncomfortable with the bloodstains on the floor. (NCSHS.)

Photographed in 1908, the Samuel I. Thornton family gathered during a family reunion at the patriarch's home, the Harper House. Sam was described as eccentric, farming his land using tenants, field hands, and his sons while he spent his time horse trading in nearby stores. Thornton's widow, Susan "Jane" Kennedy Thornton, occupied the house following his death in 1912 until her 1921 demise. From left to right are (first row, kneeling) Penny Thornton, Allie Morris Barfield, Bessie Thornton, Jim Thornton, Lettie Thornton, Effie Thornton, Arthur Thornton, and unidentified but possibly Ava H. Thornton; (second row) Fannie Morris Thornton, Minnie Thornton, Grady Thornton, Sallie Cole (sitting), Jane Thornton (sitting), and Samuel Thornton (sitting); (third row, standing) Penny Langston, Alonzo Thornton with baby Facie Thornton, Pherbee Thornton, Mary Thornton, Lula Morris with baby Luna Morris, Elijah Morris with baby Walter Morris, Betty Thornton with unidentified baby, Samuel "Dock" Thornton, Bill Joyner, James "Bob" Thornton, Bowden Thornton, William "Carson" Thornton, and unidentified. (SANC.)

From left to right in this c. 1908 photograph are Alonzo Thornton, Samuel I. Thornton, James F. "Bob" Thornton, Fannie Morris Thornton, Minnie Thornton, Effie Thornton, and William "Carson" Thornton. The ladder leaning against the roof of the house was for dousing chimney fires. (Johnston County Heritage Center.)

Remus D. Dunn, pictured here in the 1930s with some of his children and grandchildren, purchased the Harper House in 1919. By the time of his death in 1943, Remus was a widower three times over. His fourth wife, Lula Morris, Sam I. Thornton's granddaughter, lived until 1966. Remus's son Jake Dunn was the next owner of the Harper House. (Larry Laboda.)

Remus Dunn added the wing on the left of the Harper House in the 1930s. Originally it housed a partially open-air kitchen (above). The discolorations on the second floor in this photograph show where the balcony had recently been removed. By 1956 (below), the addition had been enclosed to add dining space. The normalcy of this image is what is remarkable. Laundry hangs on the line, furniture for lounging sits on the porch, and an antenna for television or radio reception is attached to the roof. The casual passerby would have no clue about the horrible things that happened here in 1865, but many already knew. Buck Dunn, who was raised in the Harper House, recalled people peeping inside while the family ate. The Harper house was already an attraction before the historic site was established. (Above, Zelda Dunn; below SANC.)

This photograph is a rare 1950s view of the rear of the Harper House. The house did not have running water; instead, a hand pump brought water to the wing of the house, and a drain expelled it into the yard. The pump and drain are visible in the bottom right of the photograph. Though the house had featured electricity since the 1930s, interior restrooms were never installed. (SANC.)

The State of North Carolina purchased the Harper property in 1957, including the house and 51 acres. Two 19th-century outbuildings can be seen on the left side of this 1957 photograph. The large oaks visible in front of the house are believed to have witnessed the battle. (SANC.)

This c. 1957 photograph shows one of the outbuildings purchased along with the Harper House and property. Like many farm outbuildings, they likely had been taken apart, adapted, and moved several times across several years. The original purpose of this outbuilding was unknown, but it was determined early on that it and a similar structure nearby would be repurposed as a replica kitchen and slave dwelling. (SANC.)

Re-siding the buildings (shown here) was just one phase of the restoration of these structures. It would be years before their interiors were furnished to match their stated purposes. In the lower-right corner, a cinder block wellhouse covering a historic well is visible. (SANC.)

The Harper House served as the centerpiece of the new historic site, which was operated by the Department of Archives and History. This 1958 prerestoration photograph shows the c. 1930s addition on the west side of the house that was used as a temporary office by staff. In 1960, twenty-four-year-old Nicholas B. Bragg, fresh from graduate school at UNC, was hired to administer the restoration of the Harper House and to make plans for a museum building. Bragg was given few instructions except to restore the house to how it may have looked when it was inhabited by the Harpers. He remained with the Department of Archives and History until 1963, just long enough to see the restoration project completed. In later years, Bragg led Old Salem Museum and Gardens and became the first director of the Reynolda House Museum, both in Winston-Salem, North Carolina. (SANC.)

In 1960, workers removed the one-story porch added by the Dunn family in the 1930s and began restoring the original roof line. In these photographs, both taken that year, workers have installed scaffolding across the front and have begun pulling back the metal roofing. The kitchen addition had not yet been removed, likely due to its use as an office. Bragg recalled that his first task upon arriving in Bentonville in 1960 was to purchase a new outhouse, which can be seen in the background above. Below, the facade of the kitchen outbuilding has already been restored, and the walls of the kitchen wing are being removed. Bragg recalled the upstairs being in extremely poor condition, partially due to later residents hanging their cured meat from the ceiling, leading to numerous grease stains on the floors. (Both, SANC.)

This c. 1960 photograph above shows a scarred landscape as restoration work on the Harper House and surrounding property continued. Large equipment, like the motor grader seen at right, was used to grade and level the ground around the house. Bricks were stacked on one end of the renovated outbuilding as work was set to begin on a chimney. The brick house in the background, located across the road, was constructed by the Dunn family shortly before they sold the Harper House to North Carolina. The house remains inhabited by the Dunn family in 2023. (Above, SANC; right, NCSHS.)

Restoration work continues in this c. 1960 photograph. A worker finalizes the removal of the west wing, leaving behind the mark of the roof line and two exterior doors that predated the addition. These doors were used by residents for access to their outbuildings—kitchen access being the most important of all. The front corner room likely served as a dining area before the addition of the wing. (SANC.)

As the restoration project continued, workers next began to paint and put final touches on the siding of the house. The well in the background (right) sits adjacent to where the visitor center is now located. A metal roof remains on the Harper House—officials were awaiting additional funding before replacing the roof with a period-correct version. (SANC.)

When the Harper House was built it was placed near an intersection of a well-traveled north-south highway with an equally well-traveled east-west route. In the 20th century, this became the intersection of Harper House Road and Mill Creek Church Road. As the visitor center neared completion, this intersection was moved 150 yards east to keep visitors from crossing Mill Creek Church Road to tour the house. Former Harper House owner Jake Dunn lamented the road being moved as it limited access to the tenant house he still owned in the background of the above photograph. Below, the house sits amongst the old-growth oak grove, trees that likely witnessed the 1865 battle. (Both, SANC.)

In 1962, North Carolina Department of Archives and History's staff photographed the completed restoration work. In addition to its storied history and use as a Civil War field hospital, the architecture of the Harper House is also significant. The two-story double-pile dwelling is representative of the vernacular use of the Greek Revival style that was popular in the 1850s. (NCMOH.)

In this 1962 photograph, final touches are placed on the Harper House exterior, including a final coat of paint. Staff chose the new colors according to a paint study that revealed the house had at some point been painted white with green trim. A more recent study has proven that the green was added by later inhabitants because the house was originally painted all white. (SANC.)

While the first floor of the newly restored Harper House was used as temporary exhibit space, the Harper House Chapter of the United Daughters of the Confederacy (UDC) furnished one upstairs bedroom with 19th-century period furnishings. The program at right for the dedication of the first furnished room in the house includes speakers from the UDC and state government. The slate of speakers below included North Carolina secretary of state Thad Eure (third from right) and restoration specialist Nicholas Bragg (fourth from left). Plans to furnish the rest of the upstairs depended on additional funding from private groups like the UDC. The state hoped to furnish the downstairs as a Civil War hospital after the completion of the planned visitor center museum nearby. (Both, NCSHS.)

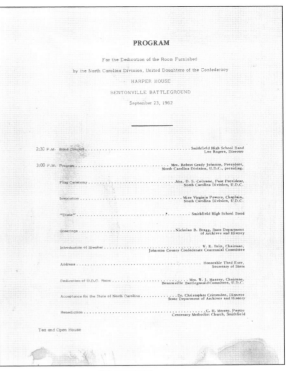

When the state purchased the Harper House in 1957, no original furniture from the Harper family remained in the home. The UDC purchased historical pieces and assisted the historic site in furnishing this bedroom (seen above and below) to show visitors how the home may have looked before the 1865 battle. The only Harper furnishing found for purchase was a pigeonholed desk used for the post office operated in the house after the Civil War (not pictured). (Both, NCSHS.)

In this 1962 photograph, visitors gather around the Harper House before and after viewing the newly restored upstairs bedroom. The interior of the Harper House saw many incremental changes as North Carolina Historic Sites, supported by the UDC, slowly found furnishing for the additional rooms in the house. (NCSHS.)

Throughout the 1960s, the Harper House Chapter of the UDC held an annual event at the Harper House commemorating Confederate Memorial Day. This photograph, most likely from the May 9, 1964, event, shows the newly restored house as visitors tour the upstairs and downstairs with cars parked in the front. (SANC.)

State representative B.P. Woodard speaks at the rededication of the Harper House in March 1979. Extensive restoration work was funded by a grant from the Historic Preservation Fund of North Carolina. From left to right, those seated behind Woodard are Richard Sawyer and Ricky Howell from North Carolina Historic Sites, Division of Archives and History's Lawrence Tice, Mildred Langston from the Harper House UDC, and Rev. H. Wayne Lee. (Johnston County Heritage Center.)

Reenactors from the 1st North Carolina Volunteers were photographed in front of the Harper House during an anniversary program in the early 1980s. The Harper House has served as the centerpiece for reenactments and other living history programs throughout the history of the site. (Johnston County Heritage Center.)

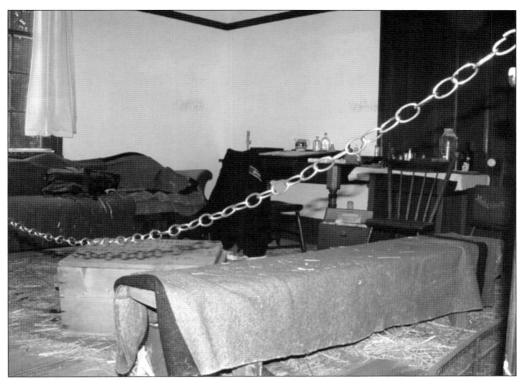

With help from the UDC and the Division of Archives and History, site staff converted all four downstairs rooms into how they may have looked when the house was in use as a hospital. The above room includes a desk with medications, a bench for minor operations, and a chain differentiating the visitor area. Below, this room is interpreted as a surgery room. An amputation kit sits on a makeshift table, while a stretcher, chloroform canisters, and other supplies sit around the room. Staff placed straw on the floor exhibiting how it may have been used to absorb blood but later removed it because it harbored termites. Both photographs were taken shortly after the 1980 interpretive change. (Both, NCSHS.)

The Harper House is no stranger to hurricanes, which are a part of life in Eastern North Carolina. Hurricane Fran made landfall near Wilmington on September 5, 1996, as a Category 3 hurricane, with sustained winds up to 115 miles per hour. Despite weakening as it moved inland, Fran's devastating effects endangered the Harper House by bringing down several old trees, some of which likely witnessed the 1865 battle. Above, it is easy to appreciate the size of one downed tree next to Lauren Cook Burgess, former president of the Bentonville Battlefield Historical Association. Years later, Hurricanes Matthew (2016) and Florence (2018) wreaked havoc on the Bentonville community due to the torrential rainfall associated with both storms. Below is one of many nearby roads washed out by Matthew. (Both, NCSHS.)

Five

ESTABLISHING A HISTORIC SITE

On August 30, 1957, Jake and Pauline Dunn signed a deed selling the Harper House and 51 acres to the State of North Carolina for $50,000. The General Assembly appropriated half of the price, Johnston County advanced $10,000, and the remaining $15,000 was raised by private donors. Pictured from left to right are Johnston County clerk of court H.V. Rose, Jake Dunn, and Pauline Dunn. (SANC.)

Born in 1887, Herschel V. Rose was born and raised in the still-recovering community of Bentonville. The Civil War was personal to Rose as his father was a Confederate soldier confined in Point Lookout prison during the battle. Rose embraced Bentonville's legacy, eventually becoming the foremost expert on the battle. Balancing a career as a farmer and clerk of court for Johnston County, Rose frequently toured the battlefield with veterans of the battle and later their descendants. Rose remained instrumental in telling the story of Bentonville and campaigning for its preservation among fellow Johnstonians. Following his 1959 death, the *Smithfield Herald* labeled him the "father of Bentonville restoration." Rose lived just long enough to see the establishment of Bentonville Battleground State Historic Site, the crowning achievement of his long life. (Johnston County Heritage Center.)

Duke's Dr. Jay Luvass (right and below left) and a representative from North Carolina Historic Sites (below right) inspect earthworks in 1957. These trenches were constructed by the 1st Regiment, Engineers and Mechanics, Michigan, on the extreme left of the Union line. Located a few hundred yards northeast of the Harper House, the Michiganders' breastworks make up a significant portion of the three miles of field fortifications remaining from the battle. (Both, SANC.)

While historians and state personnel surveyed the battlefield in 1957, they attempted to document many of the remaining breastworks built by soldiers during the battle. In several places, they were amazed to find remaining revetment logs. Soldiers on both sides would have used fence rails or logs (like the one pictured here) to reinforce their entrenchments and provide rudimentary protection for themselves during battle. (SANC.)

State personnel, along with relic hunters and visitors alike, often found artifacts while exploring the trenches in the woods near the site. In this 1960 photograph, an unidentified man shows off a complete bayonet likely found in the trenches purchased by the state in 1957. (NCSHS.)

In this 1960s photograph, state archeologists search for artifacts on the newly acquired property. Metal-detecting for relics by amateurs had become a popular pastime and drew enthusiasts from across the state to Bentonville to search for remnants of the battle including bullets, belt buckles, buttons, and more. Sadly, records on where artifacts were found were poorly kept if at all. It is now illegal to metal-detect on state property. (NCMOH.)

Many fascinating artifacts were found at Bentonville in the 20th century, but none more so than this Model 1850 staff and field officer's sword owned by Lt. Col. Samuel Tolles of the 15th Connecticut. The sword is remarkable because neither Tolles nor the 15th fought at Bentonville. Tolles and most of his regiment had been captured near Kinston on March 8. (Authors' collection.)

As news spread of the purchase of the property, visitors began to flock to see the new historic site, reviving interest in the mostly forgotten battle. This photograph of an unidentified boy pointing at the 1895 Goldsboro Rifles monument in 1957 shows the work that still needed to be done, with weeds growing out of the base. (NCMOH.)

Siblings Marjorie and Bobby Bass from Bentonville represented the Harper House Chapter of the United Daughters of the Confederacy in the Confederate Centennial Festival parade in Raleigh in 1961. The North Carolina Confederate Centennial celebrated the "Lost Cause" and attempted to reframe the Civil War as solely a fight for states' rights. Events like these neglected many of the controversial or difficult aspects of Civil War memory like slavery. (NCMOH.)

The Department of Archives and History printed this small booklet to promote Bentonville Battleground State Historic Site in 1962. The booklet provides a history of the battle and advertises the newly opened Harper House as being "available to school and club groups for special tours." The booklet is one example of how staff attempted to capitalize on the national interest generated by the Civil War centennial. (NCSHS.)

This photograph captures most of the Bentonville Battleground State Historic Site as it was in 1962. The Harper House is visible in the background behind the Goldsboro Rifles monument. This scene can no longer be recreated due to the construction of the visitor center and the relocation of Mill Creek Church Road. To the right behind the monument is the rest of the park including the first preserved trenches. (NCMOH.)

Photographed from Harper House Road, one of 29 historical markers erected in 1963 sits in front of the Goldsboro Rifles monument. Like the monument, the sign claims 360 Confederates are buried here. From 2007 to 2011, a series of modern archaeological surveys instead found evidence of 20 to 30 graves near the monument. Hundreds more likely remain buried on the battlefield in unmarked locations, making Bentonville one vast cemetery. (NCMOH.)

To help direct visitors to the new historic site, the Department of Archives and History partnered with the Smithfield Rotary Club and the State Highway and Public Works Department in 1963 to install interpretive plaques at the Interstate 95 rest areas in Johnston County. Signage was also installed by the Highway Department (the forerunner of today's Department of Transportation) directing people to the Harper House from Interstate 95. (SANC.)

While the Bentonville Advisory Committee raised the necessary funds to construct a new visitor center and museum, the four rooms downstairs in the Harper House served as a temporary exhibit space for visitors to learn about the battle of Bentonville. In the 1962 photograph above, staff place an exhibit panel highlighting the contending officers in the battle just above one of the original fireplace mantels. A campaign map showing the routes of both armies (below) was mounted next to a built-in cabinet. (Both, SANC.)

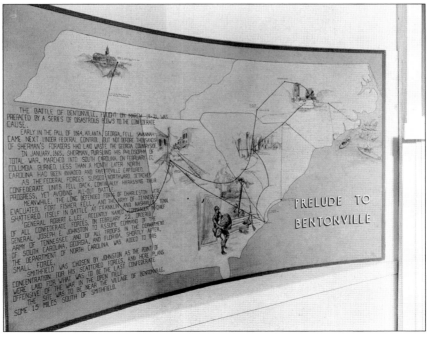

The battlefield exhibits in the Harper House were a stopgap measure until a new visitor center was completed. These exhibits included maps utilizing aerial photographs describing the actions of March 19 and March 20–21 (above). A panoramic battle scene imagined by an artist was displayed in one of the rooms (below). Space limitations prevented the staff from adequately interpreting the battle until a visitor center was built. (Both, SANC.)

The State of North Carolina opened bids to contractors in 1963 for the Bentonville visitor center and museum. The Bentonville Advisory Committee spent years raising funds to cover the projected cost of $40,000. Pictured here during construction in 1964, the visitor center featured contemporary design by Ingram and Johnson, an architect and engineering firm out of Charlotte, North Carolina. The original design of the visitor center included over 1,100 square feet of exhibit space, a 40-person lecture hall, office and storage space, and restrooms. The chosen site was less than 100 yards from the Harper House but across Mill Creek Church Road. (Both, NCSHS.)

Historic Sites staff install one of the exhibits in the Bentonville Battleground visitor center. The new visitor center featured exhibits on the lead-up to the battle, the battle itself, and its aftermath. This display focused on the various Union and Confederate generals who were involved directly or indirectly at Bentonville. (SANC.)

Another exhibit installed in the new visitor center highlighted the end of the Civil War. This panel features large text describing Gen. Joseph Johnston's surrender to Maj. Gen. William Sherman at Bennett Place roughly a month following the Battle of Bentonville. Large text panels on wood paneling were a common exhibit technique during the 1960s. (SANC.)

At right, an unidentified North Carolina Historic Sites employee or volunteer poses with a Civil War musket before placing it into the exhibits in this 1964 photograph. The wall behind her reads "Bentonville," serving as a grand introduction to the visitor center exhibits. In an attempt to create a more immersive experience, designers included the three-dimensional ground in front that eventually included stacked muskets (below). (Both, SANC.)

The centerpiece of the new exhibits was this extremely detailed diorama of the battle, which showed terrain features and had scale models of the houses that existed in Bentonville during the battle. The diorama was retired in 1999, but many visitors still ask about it today. (SANC.)

The visitor center opened in October 1964 followed by a grand opening in March. The exterior included a looped driveway to both Harper House and Mill Creek Church Roads. Staff members have quipped "somewhere there is a bus station that looks like a museum," but this architectural style was quite common. In retrospect, the Bentonville design was a modest version of the National Park Service's Mission 66 visitor center program. (SANC.)

Six

PROGRAMS AND EVENTS

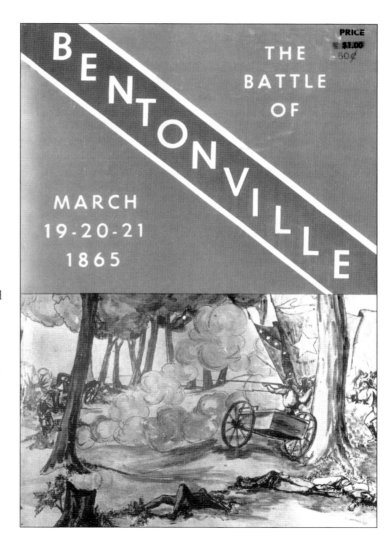

Bentonville Battleground State Historic Site had just eight short years from its inception to prepare for the 100th anniversary of the battle, which was in March 1965. The booklet pictured here served as both the first published history of the battle available for purchase and as a program for the centennial. Dr. Jay Luvass contributed the historical sketch of the battle. (NCSHS.)

On March 21, 1965, the 100th anniversary of the battle's final day, the Bentonville centennial was commemorated. Approximately 6,000 visitors gathered to see the historic weapons demonstrations and witness the grand opening of the visitor center. The reenactors that day included the Rebel Guard, who traveled all the way from Tyler, Texas. (SANC.)

The keynote speaker during the centennial program was US senator Ralph Yarborough of Texas, who was present due to the unveiling of a Texas monument at Bentonville that same afternoon. Other dignitaries included Yarborough's Senate colleagues from North Carolina, Sam J. Ervin Jr. and B. Everett Jordan (seated, right). State treasurer Edwin Gill also spoke during the festivities. (SANC.)

The Boy Scouts of America's Tuscarora Council commemorated the 100th anniversary of the battle of Bentonville with an "Anniversary Camporee" in 1965. Scouts received this patch for participation in the event. The Tuscarora Council, No. 424, later moved its camp near the battlefield. (NCSHS.)

As staff continued to develop the site in the 1970s, a distinction was made between the "historic" and "modern" areas. This view from the side of the Harper House depicts the modern area, including the parking lot, picnic area, and visitor center. The historic area, featuring the Harper House and outbuildings, began at the end of the sidewalk. (NCSHS.)

In this c. 1980 photograph, site staff perform maintenance duties near the site's visitor center. This area included amenities such as picnic tables and a Pepsi machine for visitors to enjoy under the shade of pecan trees. Picnic shelters were later added to the property. (NCSHS.)

Reenactors, part of the 1st North Carolina Volunteers/11th North Carolina Regiment, take a break during a site living history event on October 15, 1978, photographed by site manager Jack Rose. From left to right are Matthew Brady, Rick Moon, Bill Potts, Hugh Crummey, Dennis Cooley, and Melvin Lane. (NCSHS.)

In March 1980, Dr. Larry E. Tise, director of the North Carolina Division of Archives and History (standing), presented the board game created by 17-year-old Erik D. France (not pictured) of Durham. Although the game received positive reviews, only 1,000 copies were printed. Seated left to right are Attorney General Rufus Edmisten of North Carolina, North Carolina Historic Sites administrator Richard Sawyer, and Rev. H. Wayne Lee. (NCSHS.)

Following the presentation of the Bentonville game, Attorney General Edmisten spoke in conjunction with the rededication of the Goldsboro Rifles monument. Following an extensive refurbishment, the restored monument was unveiled as part of the 1980 commemoration of the battle. During his remarks, Edmisten spoke to the "bravery of all soldiers who fought in the Civil War Battle of Bentonville." (NCSHS.)

The first annual Battle of Bentonville commemoration and tactical demonstration occurred on March 22 and 23, 1980, the 115th anniversary of the battle. A family can be seen in this image walking through "camp" between the visitor center and Harper House during the program. Reenactors from the 1st North Carolina Volunteers/11th North Carolina Regiment conducted weapons demonstrations and other living history activities. (NCSHS.)

Staff member Rob Boyette (center right) speaks to representatives from the Sons of Confederate Veterans (SCV) while a reenactor looks on in this 1982 image. The SCV donated two brick entrance columns that were placed on the Mill Creek Church Road entrance to the site. The word "Bentonville" was on the left column, and "Battleground" was on the right. Eventually, this would become the primary entrance to the Harper House/visitor center area. (NCSHS.)

The site's flagpoles can be seen in this early-1980s image of reenactors lounging in front of the visitor center. From left to right, the flags are a Confederate Third National, a modern US, and a North Carolina flag. Bentonville's new entrance sign (center) and a country store (left) can be seen in the background. (NCSHS.)

A visitor departs the historic site heading east toward the battlefield during an early-1980s special event. Until 2004, the "driving tour" of the battlefield consisted solely of historical markers placed along the roadside by the Department of Archives and History during the early 1960s. Heavy traffic on Harper House Road made it extremely dangerous for tourists to stop and read this signage. (NCSHS.)

The first annual Bentonville Battleground History Bowl, sponsored by the Harper House Chapter of the United Daughters of the Confederacy (UDC), was held near the Harper House in 1981. History Bowl was the brainchild of Bentonville employee Rob Boyette, who is on the front of the stage. He is joined by Jim McPherson from the North Carolina Historic Sites home office and teams from Pine Level and Erwin Elementary Schools. (NCSHS.)

The second annual History Bowl was held behind the Harper House in 1982. From its origins at Bentonville, the History Bowl grew into a statewide event that challenged eighth graders on their knowledge of Civil War and North Carolina history. In this photograph, staff member Elaine Dunn quizzes the two teams. (NCSHS.)

Tactical demonstrations conducted by the 1st North Carolina Volunteers/11th North Carolina Regiment were a common site in the 1980s at Bentonville Battleground. Reenactors and living historians remained active in the events and programming at the site, participating in multiple demonstrations a year, including the annual anniversary commemoration. In this 1982 image, reenactors fire muskets and a cannon while another portrays a casualty of battle. (NCSHS.)

The site hosted the fourth annual living history and tactical demonstration on November 3 and 4, 1984. In this photograph, reenactors portray a Civil War–era Confederate horn band while infantry marches in the background. (Johnston County Heritage Center.)

A young visitor walks through the extensive living history encampments in front of the Harper House during the 1984 reenactment. More than 600 reenactors participated in the event, which included camp life displays, civilian life displays, sutlers selling historical goods, and more. (NCSHS.)

An unidentified staff member or volunteer enjoys a cigarette in the Bentonville gift shop located inside the visitor center in the early 1980s, while an elderly reenactor portraying a US officer stands in the foreground. Flags, miniature cannons, and toy soldiers were sold from a sales desk operated by the Harper House Chapter of the UDC and located at the front of the visitor center. (NCSHS.)

Mildred Langston (right) sits behind the sales desk ready to sell Bentonville Battleground t-shirts in the mid-1980s. Langston was a leader of the Harper House Chapter of the UDC and a longtime volunteer at the site. Fellow volunteer David Henkel (below) also poses in the sales area for this 1984 photograph. When the visitor center was remodeled in 1999, the sales desk was converted to an office, and a proper gift shop area was created near the back of the building adjacent to the exhibit area. The UDC was a partner in the site's gift shop well into the 21st century. (Both, NCSHS.)

In 1986, gift shop proceeds earned by the Harper House Chapter of the UDC allowed it to purchase at auction a full-scale firing replica of a 3-inch ordnance rifle. The cannon was presented to the site at a ceremony (above) that was photographed from the balcony of the Harper House, conspicuous by the yellow hospital flag in the foreground. Below, staff member Cliff Tyndall and Harper House UDC members Mildred Langston (center) and Pauline Beasley Davis (right) pose in front of the newly purchased artillery piece. Site staff still use this cannon during living history events today. (Both, NCSHS.)

Civil War medicine and the Harper House were the focus of the March 1987 anniversary living history program. Visitors queue while waiting their turn to see the Harper House, which featured reenactors portraying Civil War medical personnel and wounded soldiers. (NCSHS.)

Juxtaposed to the Harper House during the 1987 anniversary was a modern US Navy/Marine Corps forward field hospital from Camp Lejeune. After seeing living historians recreate an 1865 military hospital, visitors were able to learn about 1980s battlefield medicine. In this photograph, marines portray wounded soldiers before and after treatment. (NCSHS.)

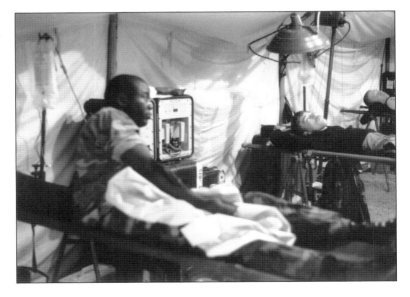

A mule-drawn wagon (above) brings "wounded" soldiers to the Harper House for treatment during the 1987 anniversary program. Staff members (below) awaited the arrival of the wounded from the field to administer treatment. Assistant site manager Cliff Tyndall (left) acted as a Union army captain and surgeon, while Morris Bass (right) was his hospital steward. Reenactor Gary Arnold from the 1st/11th North Carolina portrayed the wounded soldier receiving treatment. Stewards served many functions in Civil War hospitals from administration to pharmacy to nursing. Notice the bottle of chloroform on the table next to the wounded soldier. Ninety-five percent of surgeries during the Civil War were conducted under anesthesia, something site staff have long attempted to accurately portray. (Both, NCSHS.)

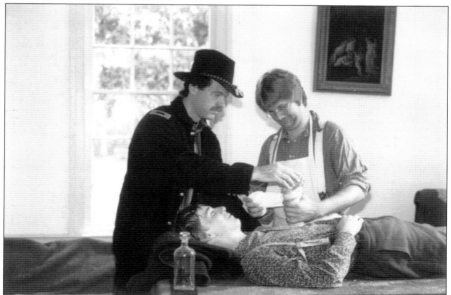

Military visits to Bentonville, which began informally during World War II, became official with the arrival of "staff rides" to Bentonville in the 1980s. A staff ride is a visit by members of the military for a specialized tour that they essentially give through individuals or groups assuming the role of a participant in the battle. Staff members ride along to facilitate discussions, but it is important that the soldiers or marines do most of the talking. In 1986, US Army soldiers arrived for their staff ride (above) in Black Hawk helicopters. The Airborne soldiers, conspicuous in their berets, were shown around the battlefield by a staff member (below). (Both, NCSHS.)

Children cover their ears as their parents watch a living history demonstration (above) in front of the Harper House on September 1, 1987. This image has been duplicated many times over the years during programs at Bentonville. Below, a musket salute is photographed beside the Goldsboro Rifles monument during the Confederate Memorial Day commemoration on May 13, 1988. The proliferation of these living history activities in the 1980s set the stage for the programs that Bentonville still conducts today. Visitors who were brought to Bentonville as children in the 1980s now bring their own children to watch 19th-century weapons demonstrations. (Both, Johnston County Heritage Center.)

Because most of the original trenches at Bentonville remained on private property in the 1980s, replica breastworks were constructed to help educate the public about Civil War combat. The recreated fortifications included an artillery platform that could be utilized during living history events to hold the site's ordnance rifle. Pictured from left to right are assistant manager Cliff Tyndall and reenactors Robert Tyndall, Billy Tanner, and Gary Riggs. (NCSHS.)

Volunteer David Henkel portrays a Union infantryman for a school group in the field fortification exhibit during a field trip in the mid-1980s. These exhibit trenches were constructed across Mill Creek Church Road from the visitor center, just north of the Harper family cemetery. This area was also the entrance to the site's short walking trail that connected the replica works to authentic Union trenches from the battle. (NCSHS.)

Building on the successful living history programs of the 1980s, the site began hosting full-scale battle reenactments every five years beginning in 1990. Photographed here in March 1995, the second reenactment, commemorating the battle's 130th anniversary, featured 1,800 reenactors and had approximately 27,000 spectators over two days. Reenactments have continued to grow in size and popularity every five years. (NCSHS.)

Bentonville site manager John Goode (far left) and Lauren Cook-Burgess (far right) of the Bentonville Battleground Historical Association welcome board members from the Johnston County Visitors Bureau to Bentonville in 1996 to commemorate the county's 250th anniversary. From left to right, the board members are Hank Daniels, Ron Sloan, Melissa Oliver, Sue Dupree, Shannon Hinnant, Earl Creech, Nonnie Dillehay, and Mike Fleming. (NCSHS.)

Seven

BENTONVILLE IN
THE 21ST CENTURY

Bentonville entered the 21st century with a remodeled visitor center and a new name. "Battleground" was replaced by "Battlefield" to reflect site growth. Photographed cutting the ribbon to the new visitor center in 1999, from left to right, are manager John Goode, the UDC's Debra Westbrook, Department of Cultural Resources' Dr. Jeff Crow, North Carolina Historic Sites' James McPherson, Department of Cultural Resources secretary Betty Ray McCain, and the Bentonville Battlefield Historical Association's Phil Shaw. (NCSHS.)

Visitors queue to get a view of the new exhibits in the visitor center following the formal dedication of the remodeled building in August 1999. The remodeled visitor center included brand-new exhibits and a $30,000 fiber-optic map depicting troop movements on the first day of the battle. Site staff worked out of the Harper House during the remodel just as their predecessors had 40 years earlier. (NCSHS.)

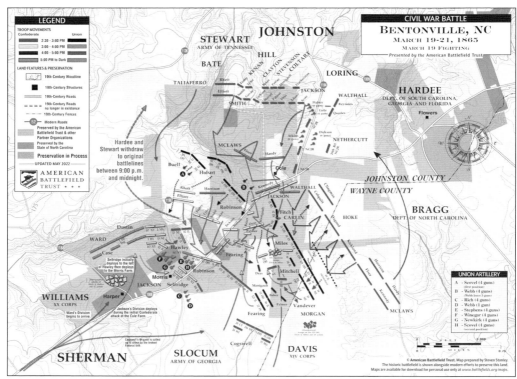

For nearly 50 years, Bentonville Battlefield State Historic Site grew in popularity but not in size. Expansion was limited to a few isolated tracts during the 1980s and 1990s. This changed in the 2000s largely through the auspices of the Civil War Preservation Trust (later rebranded as the American Battlefield Trust) and like-minded organizations. Roughly 2,000 acres have now been preserved, approximately one-third of the 6,000-acre battlefield. (American Battlefield Trust.)

More change came in 2000 with the naming of Donny Taylor as site manager. Taylor's background as both a farmer and a reenactor made him a perfect candidate to lead Bentonville into the new century. He is seen here with NPS chief historian emeritus Ed Bearss during a tour of the Cole Plantation. Bearss was a longtime champion of preservation efforts at Bentonville, especially the miles of extant earthworks. (NCSHS.)

One of Donny's mandates as manager was to preserve and improve the historic site's relationship with the Bentonville community. Two pillars of Bentonville were photographed flanking site maintenance mechanic Bobby Jones in this 2004 image. On the left is Buck Dunn, who grew up in the Harper House, and on the right is Tim Westbrook, the unofficial "mayor" of Bentonville. (NCSHS.)

With expansion came the installation of tour stops allowing visitors to access the battlefield without the dangers that came with pulling off on the side of the road. In this 2004 photograph, contractors pour asphalt at a tour stop soon to be christened "Morgan's Stand." The first four tour stops were opened in time for the 140th anniversary of the battle in 2005. (NCSHS.)

A Civil War Trails wayside was photographed with a combine in the background at the Merging of the Union Armies tour stop. In partnership with the historic site, the Harper House UDC, and the Johnston County Visitors Bureau, Civil War Trails installed 12 waysides across Johnston County interpreting the Carolinas Campaign. These waysides were dedicated during Bentonville's 140th anniversary commemorations. Over 1,500 Civil War Trails sites exist nationally. (NCSHS.)

A helmeted assistant site manager, Fred Burgess, poses atop a US Marine Corps light armored vehicle during a 2006 staff ride. Dozens of military groups visit Bentonville every year to continue their training, but most arrive in vans and buses instead of tanks and armored personnel carriers. (NCSHS.)

Marines from Camp Lejeune's 2nd Light Armored Reconnaissance Battalion were photographed at the Confederate High Tide tour stop during their 2006 staff ride. Staff rides are especially valuable for young military leaders as they are forced to put themselves in the shoes of their predecessors to gain a better understanding of decision-making during a battle. (NCSHS.)

In 2013, site manager Donny Taylor points out a revetment log, a piece of fence rail or other wood used by soldiers to reinforce trenches. Well-preserved revetment logs are a rare find on Civil War battlefields, but several of these can be seen along the Army of Tennessee line on the Cole Plantation. This was one of the first property acquisitions outside the Harper House area. (NCSHS.)

In 2011, Bentonville Battlefield received a unique donation, a Confederate Read artillery shell embedded in wood. Johnston County Schools donated the artifact after it was exhibited in a local school as a novelty for many years. Upon acquisition, it was determined the shell was still "live," and shockingly, staff removed cigarette butts from the fuse. Demolition experts at Camp Lejeune disarmed the shell, and once deemed safe, the site placed the artifact on display. (Authors' collection.)

140TH ANNIVERSARY REENACTMENT

BENTONVILLE BATTLEFIELD

MARCH 19–20, 2005

Hugely popular reenactments were undertaken at Bentonville in 2005 and 2010 to mark the 140th and 145th anniversaries of the battle. Above, the Johnston County Visitors Bureau released this poster to publicize Bentonville reenactments. The visitors bureau estimated that $4.5 million was spent locally by reenactors and visitors during the 2005 event, and funds raised by selling concessions at the event that year allowed the Bentonville Volunteer Fire Department to purchase a jaws of life. Below, Gary Riggs portrays a US Army surgeon in front of the Harper House during a "school day," held just before the 2010 reenactment. Hundreds of Johnston and Sampson County schoolchildren rotated through seven different living history stations that varied from sewing to cannon firings. The 2010 reenactment was the kick-off to the Department of Cultural Resources' Civil War sesquicentennial commemorations. (Both, NCSHS.)

Bentonville's 150th anniversary reenactment capitalized on the attention brought to the Civil War by the state and national sesquicentennial commemorations. What started in the 1970s with dozens of reenactors and hundreds of visitors grew to astronomical proportions. Over 60,000 people visited Bentonville during a three-day period in March 2015, a fraction of which can be seen in this aerial photograph taken on March 21, 2015. (Charles and Mike Ballard.)

North Carolina governor Pat McCrory returns the salute of reenactors who were marching in review after the March 21, 2015, "Fight for the Morris Farm" battle scenario. Over 3,000 reenactors attended the event, some traveling from as far away as Europe. Over McCrory's right shoulder is James Lighthizer, then president of the Civil War Trust. In the event shirt to McCrory's left is Keith Hardison, then the North Carolina Historic Sites division director. (NCSHS.)

Several archaeological investigations have taken place at Bentonville in the 21st century, two of which are shown here. In the above photograph, taken on an extremely cold January day in 2008, assistant state archaeologist John Mintz helps dig a test pit near the Goldsboro Rifles monument. The previous year, ground-penetrating radar hinted at graves in the area, but not a mass grave like the monument implies. The dig confirmed at least 20 graves interred individually instead of a mass burial pit. Below from left to right are volunteer Doug Williams and North Carolina Historic Sites deputy director Dale Coats digging, while site manager Donny Taylor watches on, during a 2014 archaeological search for original Harper outbuildings. Some kitchen debris and scraps were found near the reproduction kitchen but not enough to point to an exact location for the original. (Both, NCSHS.)

In 2011, Bentonville supporter Dean Harry (far right) founded the Friends of Bentonville Battlefield, Inc. (FoBB), a nonprofit whose mission is the "preservation of the memory, the spirit, and the physical condition of Bentonville Battlefield, located near the town of Four Oaks in Johnston County, North Carolina." Joining Dean in this 2013 photograph are, from left to right, fellow FoBB board members Doug Elwell, Frank Hall, and Doug Williams. (NCSHS.)

The first event sponsored by the FoBB was the "North Carolina, 1865" symposium, which was held at Johnston Community College on September 14, 2013. The impressive lineup of speakers included, from left to right, Bert Dunkerly, Dr. Chris Fonvielle, Ed Bearss, Dr. Mark Bradley, Eric Wittenberg, and FoBB vice president Col. (Ret.) Wade Sokolosky, all seen here mimicking Bearss's charge. The following day, attendees toured Bentonville with Bearss and Bradley. (NCSHS.)

Even with the expansion of the historic site, the Harper House remains an important part of the Bentonville story. In 2012, site staff partnered with forensic scientist Dr. James Bailey from UNC-Wilmington (above left) and Dr. Max Noureddine of ForensiGen, LLC (above right), to sample floor stains to determine if they were caused by blood, which proved to be the case. Site manager Donny Taylor (center) kneels with the two scientists. Below, the Harper House was interpreted as a working hospital during "War So Terrible," a living history program that took place in October 2014. Nighttime tours of the Harper House are extremely popular and routinely sell out. (Both, NCSHS.)

In October 2017, Bentonville Battlefield unveiled a new walking trail allowing visitor access to the Cole Plantation, the site of intense fighting during the battle. Photographed from left to right are Dean Harry and Donna Bailey-Taylor from the FoBB; staff members Jeff Fritzinger, Amanda Brantley, Donny Taylor, Chad Jefferds, and Derrick Brown; North Carolina Historic Sites division staff Jeff Bockert and Chuck LeCount; and historian Dr. Mark Bradley. (NCSHS.)

Following the trail's grand opening, Dr. Mark Bradley (left), author of *Last Stand in the Carolinas: The Battle of Bentonville*, leads a tour of the Cole Plantation. Photographed from left to right, Bradley is joined by Wade Sokolosky, Dean Harry, Chuck LeCount, Jeff Bockert, and Pattie Smith. Sokolosky and Harry are Bentonville tour guides in their own right, while Pattie succeeded Dean as president of the FoBB in 2020. (NCSHS.)

Maintenance mechanic Johnny Carter instructs volunteers on the cleaning of tombstones in this April 2011 photograph. The volunteers were members of the Civil War Trust who were on site for Park Day, an annual historic site cleanup day sponsored nationally by the trust. While these volunteers cleaned the markers in the Harper cemetery, others were cleaning the site's walking trails. (NCSHS.)

FoBB board member Doug Elwell poses in March 2013 with the newly arrived monument to Union troops that participated in the battle. Elwell served as a fundraiser for the monument in his capacity as a member of the Sons of Union Veterans of the Civil War. The monument was purchased through donations, a sizable portion of which were collected in the 1990s during the first Union monument campaign. (NCSHS.)

In 2018, Bentonville community members convened in the visitor center to express their opinions about the future of the battlefield. The forum was an important part of the strategic planning process for the site and was sponsored by the FoBB. Charles Page from the Cool Springs Center (standing) was the moderator for the event. It was special for Bentonville's staff to hear how important the battlefield was to the community. (NCSHS.)

The new strategic plan was unveiled during "Two Weeks of Fury," a symposium that took place in April 2019 after being postponed by Hurricane Florence. The biggest takeaway from the plan was the need for a new visitor center to replace the 1960s structure Bentonville has now. In this image, newly appointed site manager Colby Stevens addressed the audience before keynote speakers Dr. Craig Symonds and Dr. John Marzlak spoke. (NCSHS.)

Musician and radio host Rissi Palmer, who traces her roots to Bentonville, performed near the Harper House in 2020 during the COVID-19 pandemic with guitarist James Gilmore for North Carolina Historic Sites' "Singing on the Land" initiative. Palmer and Gilmore performed Allison Russell's "Barley," which Palmer chose because "I think about my ancestors, and I feel them and it doesn't make me sad, it fills me with a lot of pride." (Authors' collection.)

Although a key piece of the battlefield story, the bullpen area of the battlefield long remained inaccessible due to private ownership and rough terrain. In 2023, that decades-long dream became a reality as the site, partnering with the North Carolina Mountains-to-Sea Trail and the FoBB, opened the Bull Pen Trail. Photographed at the trail opening, visitors Carolyn Cole and Norma Jean Gore discuss the battle with guide Wade Sokolosky. (North Carolina Department of Natural and Cultural Resources.)

DISCOVER THOUSANDS OF LOCAL HISTORY BOOKS
FEATURING MILLIONS OF VINTAGE IMAGES

Arcadia Publishing, the leading local history publisher in the United States, is committed to making history accessible and meaningful through publishing books that celebrate and preserve the heritage of America's people and places.

Find more books like this at
www.arcadiapublishing.com

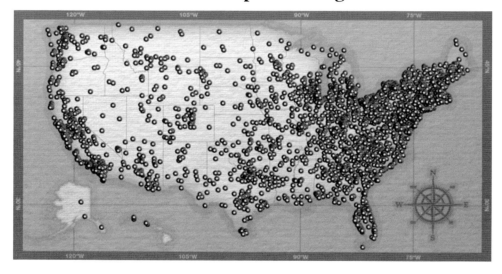

Search for your hometown history, your old stomping grounds, and even your favorite sports team.

Consistent with our mission to preserve history on a local level, this book was printed in South Carolina on American-made paper and manufactured entirely in the United States. Products carrying the accredited Forest Stewardship Council (FSC) label are printed on 100 percent FSC-certified paper.

MADE IN THE